Today Is A Great Day To Be Positive
My Gratitude Journal. Pink, Orange and Green Motivational Journal For Women
Paperback ISBN: 978-1-989733-40-0
Copyright Dunhill Clare Publishing 2020
All Rights Reserved. Cover Design by Sharon Purtill

www.ingramcontent.com/pod-product-compliance
Lightning Source LLC
Chambersburg PA
CBHW070150080526
44586CB00015B/1919